CRYSTAL PA
SPEEDW

The Thrills and Spills of the ___ ___ ___

by LIONEL CROSSLEY

Edited by KEITH WYNCOLL and ALISON EDWARDS

Crystal Palace Foundation (c) 1986

Lionel Crossley

Lionel Crossley was a 'novice' speedway rider with Crystal Palace from 1933-34 and in 1939. He also rode at Dagenham Amateur track between these periods and at several local grass tracks. Since the early 1950s he has been an Auto Cycle Union timekeeper and is actively involved in a speedway training track for young riders at Iwade, Kent. He is a member of the Veteran Speedway Riders Association and the Crystal Palace Foundation.

Acknowledgements

I should like to place on record my grateful thanks to Keith Wyncoll and Alison Edwards for encouraging me to write this book and for the countless hours they spent in producing it. Many of my speedway friends have given me support and historical advice, particularly Len Cole, Fred Cooper, Ron Hoare, Roy Etches, Frank North and other members of the Veteran Dirt Track Riders' Association. Thanks also for the use of photographs from Mrs Cyril May, Eric Price, Ron Hoare, Ken Talbot (Talbot collection) and the C.P.F. archives.

This publication grew out of the work of the C.P.F. Palace Memories Group who gather the memories of people like me who knew and enjoyed the Crystal Palace.

LIONEL CROSSLEY.

Design and Layout - Mick Gilbert
Word processing - Bill Bourne
Artwork - Keith Wyncoll and
          Alison Edwards
Printer - Elan Printing

ISBN No. 0 9508334 3 6

Published by the Crystal Palace Foundation, 84 Anerley Road, London SE19 2AH.

CONTENTS

Foreword

I am particularly pleased to recommend Lionel Crossley's book as what I believe is a valuable addition to the published record of dirt-track and speedway racing history.

Cyril J. Hart*
Former editor of 'Speedway World',
Former Secretary of the
Speedway Riders' Association,
Member of the Veteran Speedway
Riders' Association

George Newton

MORE POWER TO YOUR TWIST GRIP!

Have you ever fancied your chances of becoming a speedway rider? You have? Well, you have taken the first of a number of expensive decisions.

Approximately 15 to 20 weeks' wages should see you kitted out with leathers, helmet, boots, gloves, one steel shoe, a pair of good quality goggles, body belt and back protector and a fairly good second hand machine in raceable condition. (It also took about the same number of weeks wages way back in 1930-34). Transport will also be needed for the machine since it must not be ridden on the public highway.

A visit to the local training track prior to beginning training will not go amiss, just to see how other young hopefuls are coping. Get to know some of the officials, find out whether methanol engine fuel ('dope') and oil are available and how much they cost. Check out what training is given, how much this costs and when it is available. If possible try to get accustomed to the controls and general handling of the new machine in a farmer's field or the local track car park because you will find the performance is quite phenomenal, and no brakes are fitted to help you stop. A well equipped toolbox and a few special tools for your particular machine are necessary, as is some form of insurance. Your training track instructor will advise you on this, but it is a must. Having satisfied yourself on all these matters, present yourself at the track for your first spin. Before riding there are a few things still to be checked such, as tyre pressures, gearing etc. Speedway machines have fixed gears (i.e. they are not fitted with a gearbox). The only way to change gear ratio is by changing the engine sprocket, and/or the rear wheel sprocket and then re-adjusting the two chains for correct tension.

Have you mastered the 'run and bump' start yet? Pull the machine backwards until the compression stroke is encountered, pull in the clutch, push the machine whilst running alonside at a fair speed and jump sideways onto the saddle at the same time releasing the clutch whilst slightly opening the throttle. With luck it will fire and you can then get onto the saddle properly whilst pulling the clutch lever. The machine can then be stopped with the feet, but at least the motor is running. Check that the oil is being pumped via the oil pump sight feed, that the fuel taps are in the 'ON' position, and settle yourself comfortably. You are now more or less ready for your first ride. Simple isn't it?

Following several slow laps, the instructor will suggest a few practice starts. The engine revs should be built up to a near maximum and with your nerves strained and tingling you await the starting signal. Release the clutch as quickly as is appropriate, since the whole machine will seem to want to turn over backwards. Downwards pressure on the handlebars keeps things on an even keel and the bike and rider are launched forward at an alarming rate. In what seems no time at all, the safety fence surrounding the first bend looms up ahead and you have no brakes to slow down with.

Remembering the instructor's words, you take your life in your hands, and lay the machine over to the left at what seems an unnecessary angle until you feel that the front wheel is breaking adhesion... Help! At this stage a little more throttle causes the back wheel to start sliding, bringing the front wheel more or less upright and thus under some sort of control. The left leg pushed forward helps to maintain balance. The amount of back wheel slide largely determines the direction of travel, and while this can be varied to a greater or lesser degree by the handlebars, these are primarily an aid to rider balance.

If you have not fallen off yet, you still have to fight three very great forces: forward propulsion or momentum provided by a motor developing upward of 50 brake horse power; centrifugal force of the rider and machine being propelled in the arc of a circle - this tends to fling the machine into the safety fence unless it is counteracted - finally, gravity tends to pull the rider and machine into the loose cinder (or shale) surface.

A shifting of rider weight and a yet smaller angle of machine lean will counteract all these forces and cause the machine to straighten up in readiness for the dash down the next straight. Here you need the maximum acceleration possible so get your weight over the back wheel for the best grip. A slight easing of the twist grip may well help here, since this reduces the amount of spin, promoting better grip.

The second bend is looming rapidly ahead, and you are travelling very much quicker than at the first bend. All that you have been taught must now be put into practice. You are probably perspiring profusely by now!

Lay the machine over, get the back sliding and steer into the slide. Shift your weight and prepare for the next straight. You have completed a whole lap. If your confidence is high, try a second lap. Be careful not to use too much throttle as this causes the back wheel to overslide, with possible devastating results. The rear end of the machine could come right round and face the wrong way, usually pitching the rider over the bars and face first into the shale. Ignominy! All this occurs at great speed, invariably accompanied by slight dizziness to the rider.

Usually the instructor will quickly arrive to see all is well, help straighten out any bent pieces on the machine, criticize what went wrong and suggest cures. Do not get too despondent. The rider who never made a mistake never made anything in his life. Be determined, get back on the machine and make another attempt. Having mastered the machine on a practice track you still have to get accepted and 'signed up' by a professional club. This is the most difficult part of the exercise and your future can depend on who you know rather than just what you know. Put your best foot forward and more power to your twist grip!

Speedway still gives me a thrill even though it is 46 years since I hung up my leathers as a Palace novice at the outbreak of war. Let me take you back to those halcyon days when path racing and later speedway thrilled huge crowds at the Crystal Palace.

Cinders fly at the pit-gate end

ALL FOR A BOB!

The Crystal Palace was a huge glass edifice designed by Sir Joseph Paxton for the Great Exhibition of 1851, and transferred in 1854 to the top of Sydenham Hill in South London. Sadly it was burned to the ground during a massive conflagration in 1936, thus bringing to an end the concerts, exhibitions, festivals and vast range of sports and entertainment of previous years. A tragic loss to thousands of pleasure seeking Londoners.

The North Tower

CRYSTAL PALACE

WHIT MONDAY

CONTINUOUS AMUSEMENT from 10 until 10

MILITARY CONCERT BY

MASSED BANDS

ASSISTED BY DRUMS, FIFES AND PIPERS OF THE

BRIGADE OF GUARDS

SPEEDWAY RACING

2 o'clock   (Organised by LONDON MOTOR SPORTS Ltd.)

GREAT OPEN-AIR

BOXING TOURNAMENT

At 3.30 p.m.   (Organised by HULLS Boxing Promotions)

THREE HOURS CONTINUOUS BOXING

GRAND DISPLAY OF BROCK'S DAYLIGHT

FIREWORKS

At the Conclusion of the Speedway Racing

CINEMA - DANCING - VAUDEVILLE
SHOWS - ETC.

ADMISSION 1/- (Plus Tax)   CHILDREN 6d. (Plus Tax)

For more than eighty years it had been a popular landmark, visible for upwards of forty miles. From the public viewing platform on top of the 280 foot North Tower, one could see to the North far beyond Alexandra Palace and Hampstead Heath on a clear day. To the South, ships could be seen, with binoculars, through a gap in the South Downs at Birling Gap. Planes such as 'Hannibal' and 'Heracles' of Imperial Airways and 'Fleche d'Or' of French Airlines could be seen at the old Croydon Airport. To the East, ships could be seen in the Thames Estuary as far as Southend pier. To the West, Hampton Court, Windsor Castle and the Thames Valley could easily be discerned.

All these fine panoramic views could be enjoyed for a modest outlay of one penny if one toiled up the 400 odd steps, or three pence if one could afford the lift. At the foot of the tower was a sizable man-made lake in which a variety of aquatic sports were performed such as water skiing,

boating and motor boat racing. This was very exciting since the spectators were allowed quite close to the water's edge. Thus, in the 30's, you could watch 'The Corinthians' in a top class amateur football match, followed by a three hour speedway match, and end the fabulous day with speedboat racing, and all for a bob (5p in today's money).

No wonder the Palace attracted such huge crowds in those pre-television days. Additional trams were employed from the top of Anerley Hill to disperse the crowds towards South Norwood, Croydon, Sutton or Mitcham. Subsequently trolley buses, and later London Transport buses replaced the trams and trolley buses. For myself, I often bemoaned the passing of the

trams which held a peculiar fascination for me, or was it simply nostalgia?

The spacious grounds had for years been the home of football, cycle racing, fairground, open air boxing etc., and many other pleasurable forms of pastime. Most of these gradually declined, the grounds became neglected, and only the Brock's fireworks displays attracted large crowds of spectators. Thus in 1926 the trustees of the Crystal Palace looked around for new ways of attracting larger numbers of spectators. Motor cycle racing was then gaining in popularity at Brooklands and many local grass track circuits in Kent, Surrey and Sussex.

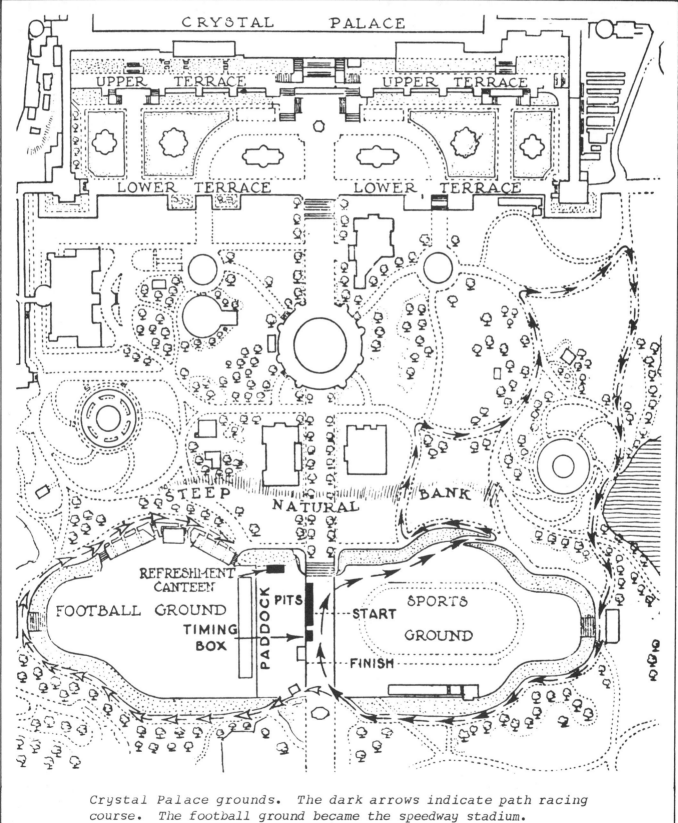

CRYSTAL PALACE

UPPER TERRACE   UPPER TERRACE

LOWER TERRACE   LOWER TERRACE

STEEP   NATURAL   BANK

REFRESHMENT
CANTEEN

FOOTBALL GROUND   PITS   SPORTS

TIMING
BOX   PADDOCK   START   GROUND

FINISH

Crystal Palace grounds. The dark arrows indicate path racing course. The football ground became the speedway stadium.

The 8th Crystal Palace Motor Cycle Race Meeting, 1928.
F.E. Parnacott 3.48 AJS, L. Lancaster 3.48 Velocette (the
winner), and E. Langman 3.48 Velocette taking the Maze
hairpin bend in the Middlesex cup event.

PATH RACING

The Crystal Palace General Manager, Sir Henry Buckland, invited the promoters of London Motor Sports to put on a Saturday afternoon motor cycle event in the grounds. Mr. Fred Mockford and Mr. Cecil Smith quickly organised the meeting with riders from the Streatham and Sydenham Motor Cycle Clubs. From this humble beginning, which attracted large crowds of spectators, emerged the Crystal Palace Path Racing meetings and these continued at monthly intervals throughout the summer until 1934.

Following a considerable advertising campaign around South London, something like twenty thousand spectators enjoyed a good afternoon of exhilarating racing. Later, when the competitors' lists were opened to riders throughout the South of England, this centre of the Auto Cycle Union encouraged spectators to flock from a wider area.

In 1927, the popular London newspaper 'Daily Sketch', offered its regular readers a gift for their offspring. This took the form of a membership card giving free admission for children up to sixteen to the Crystal Palace grounds on all days except for the Thursday firework displays. The inception of motor cycle racing and later speedway racing ensured that these cards became worth their weight in gold since the admission was sixpence for children. This fact is mentioned in passing since it helped to foster a whole new generation of youthful motor cycle sports enthusiasts who then followed the sport for many years.

Racing took place on the loose gravel footpaths throughout the grounds. A circuit of one mile had been marked out with competitors proceeding in a clockwise direction around the Palace grounds.

Most of the paths were only ten or twelve feet wide, but at the start, on top of the Penge entrance banking, the width was about forty feet which permitted a 'massed start' to all races.

The path racers took a right hand bend and then up the steep natural banking where the width of the path reduced to a mere twelve feet. 'Bunching' and minor falls were frequent here though none was really serious as speeds were comparatively low. Following several hairpin bends, the riders went downhill and skirted the lake where at least one competitor met a sudden and rather wet ending to his day. A long right hand bend took riders along the top of the old cycle track banking, to be followed by a sharp drop and then back to the start for the second or succeeding laps. In view of all these hazards, lap speeds were not very high. In fact, the fastest lap recorded was during the last meeting in 1934 by Harold Daniel on a Norton at a speed of only 33.01 mph.

Gus Kuhn   Harold Daniel

Literally hundreds of solo riders competed over the eight seasons that Path Racing was in vogue. Most of them also raced at other venues such as Brands Hatch, Layhams Farm (Kent), Rainham (Kent), Horsham (Sussex), Croydon (Surrey), etc. A few of the more illustrious solo performers were Gus Kuhn, Triss Sharp, Lionel Wills, Karl Pugh, John Adie, Wally Harris, Arthur Willimott, Joe Francis, Jock West, Harold Daniel, Dick Bellamy, Ed Cornwell, Ted Pink and Norman Cottee. (Apologies to those names I may have unwittingly omitted, but the documentary evidence after nearly sixty years is sadly incomplete and memory is becoming somewhat dimmed).

Sidecar racing soon became a great spectacle, though instead of sixteen competitors per race, only six (and sometimes only four) were permitted. In view of the track complexities, sidecar speeds seldom exceeded 30 mph, though they were exhilarating and exciting.

The most prolific performers were B. Ducker, L. Truett, A.H. Horton, J. Surtees, C. Sewell, C.P. Hayward, G. Norchi, C. Smith, F.H. Brackpool, W. Wethercott, A.Noterman and J. Middleton.

The most popular outfits were Norton, Scott, Matchless, Coventry Eagle, Triumph and Rudge.

Nowadays much of the site and paths used are occupied by the National Sports Centre with very little of the original path circuit still discernible today. Several of these solo riders later became famous on the speedway circuit at the Palace, though their sidecar brethren fared rather less successfully because the dearth of performers obviously precluded regular and diversified competition.

F.E. Parnacott 3.48 AJS, L. Lancaster 3.48 Velocette (the winner), and E. Langman taking the Maze hairpin bend in the Middlesex cup event. The 8th Race Meeting, 1928.

Path Racing (c. 1927)

Sidecar Path Racing, 1928

Eddie Brynck

THE BEGINNINGS OF DIRT TRACK RACING

At the end of 1926, following several successful 'Path' meetings, Lionel Wills, heir to the famous family tobacco fortunes, made a business cum holiday trip to Australia. Here he witnessed and was excited by the dirt track racing boom currently sweeping the country. He was introduced to Mr. John Hoskins, who had started quarter-mile racing at his Electric Light Carnival at West Maitland in 1923.

Prior to this, South Africa had inaugurated a somewhat primitive form of loose surface racing and even had a national champion in Joe Sarkis. America too had a form of dirt track racing involving a number of leading motor cycle manufacturers, chiefly Indian, Harley, American X, and Excelsior. These had sponsored works teams of riders at the many mile and half mile tracks which then abounded in the U.S.A. 'Broadsiding' or 'Power Sliding' is usually credited to Maldwyn Jones on his 1,000 c.c. big twin Excelsior. His style was quickly copied by others, notably Eddie Brynck, J. Anderson, Jim Davies, John Vance, Joe Petrali, 'Sprouts' Elder and others in the years prior to 1923.

In America, races were frequently run over five or even ten miles, whereas in Australia one mile, or four laps of the quarter mile tracks was the norm. The sport had caught the public fancy in a big way, such that when Wills returned to England he spoke very volubly to the motor cycle press of the day.

Whilst still in Australia, Wills had tried his hand at this new fangled type of motor cycle racing on cinder tracks, but with limited success. This was hardly surprising since he had to compete with Billy Lamont, Ron Johnson, Sig Schlam, Charlie Datson and 'Sprouts' Elder, all of whom had three or four years racing experience behind them. However, the dirt track bug had bitten, and Wills was determined to interest the motor cycle racing fraternity in England in this new and exhilarating sport. He returned home at Christmas 1927 and contacted Mr. Mockford and Mr. Smith of London Motor Sports who were already running the Palace Path racing meetings. They in turn interested Sir Henry Buckland, the Crystal Palace Manager, and his trustees, the London County Council. This new sport of Dirt Track Racing had therefore begun in England.

Whilst a new purpose-built track was under construction at the Palace by Richard Crittall Ltd., two or three tentative attempts were made in 1927 to hold meetings at Camberley (Surrey), Droylesden (near Manchester) and also Greenford (Middlesex). These were one-off experimental meetings which failed for one reason or another: clockwise racing at one; huge size of track at another; distance from civilization at Camberley, all

Promoters Johnny Hoskins and Jack Hill-Bailey.

failed to fire public enthusiasm.

Permission was granted to run a meeting on Sunday November 9th, 1927 by the A-CU on the condition that it was open to Ilford Motor Cycle Club members only. This posed a problem since celebrated riders from all over the country wished to compete. It was only with the greatest tact that riders were persuaded not to take the law into their own hands and participate in spite of A-CU disapproval. Approval was eventually received for an open meeting early in 1928.

The first A-CU approved dirt track meeting in England was held on the old athletics track at the rear of the Kings Oak Hotel in Epping Forest on February 19th, 1928. It had been fairly well advertised in local and technical press, and a bright sunny day augured well for the promoter, Mr. R.J. Hill Bailey of the Ilford Motor Cycle Club. Together with his wife and a few voluntary helpers they catered for about 3,000 spectators with an 11.00 a.m. start. All roads leading into the Forest were jammed tight with transport of all types from a very early hour and organisation soon became chaotic. Approximately 30,000 people arrived and all tickets were sold in a few minutes.

Thousands paid no admission fees at all and hundreds climbed into the sturdy branches of the huge beech trees which surrounded the track. This led to the track being called High Beech. It had been envisaged that all spectators would be kept behind a single stout rope around the periphery of the track, but thousands had to be allowed on the in-field area also behind a staked rope. The competitors raced on a loose cinder track through an avenue of cheering fans, much to the mixed feelings of delight and consternation of the promoter. However, the meeting was completed without serious mishap. A never to be forgotten day, but one not to be repeated. Safety and organisation had to be improved.

The racing was fast, furious and unpredictable. The first race winner was Fred Ralph, later associated with the Stamford Bridge track. He received a plaque for his efforts. Other winners were Eric Spencer, Colin Watson and Ivor Creek. After a refreshment break or a visit to the Kings Oak bar, racing resumed. The highlight of the day was a demonstration of 'broadsiding' by a few Australian riders who had just arrived in England. Keith McKay, Hilary Buchanon and Stewart St. George all then proceeded to give

High Beech with crowds on both sides of the track, 1928

Lionel Wills at the Palace pits bend.

Lloyd 'Sprouts' Elder

demonstrations of the new exciting method of riding a cinder track. The crowds were spellbound. Unlike the English riders of the earlier races who contrived not to skid or slide their machines, these fellows threw their machines into violent slides at each bend and showered the luckless spectators with damp black cinders.

The crowds loved it and clamoured for more. A second meeting was held at High Beech on Easter Monday in front of another huge crowd, and this caused a wave of new tracks to be commissioned all over the country (approximately 70 in the next twelve months).

These early meetings threw up a number of points which obviously needed modification and regulation in the future. In particular there was the haphazard method of starting races, (2) the lack of a proper safety fence between riders and spectators, (3) riders needed better leather protective gear and (4) some machines were still fitted with headlamps and other non-essential protruberances which were added dangers under racing conditions. However, a start had been made and the A-CU and the promoters quickly dealt with these deficiencies.

The first final at High Beech in 1928. Note the crowd inside and outside. The riders, left to right: Ivor Creek, Fred Ralph, Hugh Smyth, and 'Sonny' Wilson.

BELOW... 1914 F.A. Cup Final at Crystal Palace.

This panorama and the one overleaf present a continuous picture showing one

SPEEDWAY AT THE PALACE

By now the Crystal Palace track had been completed with the exception of the double sprung mesh safety fence. Training and practice sessions were held whilst this was being erected and plans were laid for an early opening to take advantage of the intense public interest in dirt track racing.

Colourful posters announced the arrival of Speedway. On Saturday May 19th 1928 at 3.30 p.m. twenty thousand people arrived by bus, tram or train. They entered by turnstiles at the Centre Transept. They then had a pleasant walk down the innumerable steps, through gardens, past statues and collonades, through the fairground and under the flying airships to the new track on the site of the old football ground. Simultaneously, at the lower end of the grounds, other throngs of expectant people were passing through the Penge entrance, mingling with cars, motor cycles and bicycles converging on the track. Another entrance was in Westwood Hill which took people past numerous tennis courts en route.

To the left of the Penge entrance, where now stands a restaurant and children's zoo, were spacious car parks with a large covered accommodation for motor cycles and bicycles. Further to the left was a ten foot high fence which hid an untended lake and lots of decaying stone prehistoric monsters, all having suffered the ravages of time and vandals. Attempts to scale this fence and thus avoid admission fees were invariably met by an irate warden who kept a silent vigil on the other side. Ouch!

Having passed through the turnstiles, after paying the sixpence for children or one shilling for adults, one mounted the thirty or so steps to the top of the huge natural banking which surrounded about two thirds of the track area. One then had the first glimpse of the racing track surrounded by large trees. It was virtually an amphitheatre with a most pleasing aspect. On the far side of the track were two sizable stands, relics of the old football Cup Final days, now resplendent in fresh coats of paint.

of the two sports grounds, together capable of accommodating 150,000.

Incidentally, the track was built around the football pitch, then currently being used by the Corinthian Amateur Football Club for weekly games which started at 2.00 p.m.

Stands and cinders

The two wooden stands had a seating capacity for about one thousand patrons each, and cost an additional shilling. Beneath these stands were the riders' changing rooms and showers, and a ballroom where frequent social gatherings were held. One stand also housed an enclosed cubicle for the referee, timekeeper and announcer. Behind these stands, on top of a considerable knoll, were the celebrated Maxim's Flying Air Ships, where for three old pence one could enjoy the thrills of flying or something much akin to it. In full flight these airships gyrated over a very considerable area at a great height in absolute silence. Further afield were the zoo, fairground, maze, gardens, ponds, statues and North Tower lake with speedboats.

The track, which had cost £5,000 to lay (today's cost would be nearer a quarter of a million pounds), was a full quarter mile circuit. It was banked at both ends with a fenced off area or pits at the Penge end. Several inches of finely graded cinders obtained

racing surface. This was rolled flat by a ten ton steam roller supplied by Frank North's father from Selhurst. Frank was to become a regular and popular performer at the track.

J. HOSKINS, RON JOHNSON, FRED MACKFORD, CHARLIE DATSON, CECIL SMITH, SIG SCHLAM
Crystal Palace—Easter 1928

Pre-meeting music blared forth from several loudspeakers dotted around the stadium. The 'Skaters Waltz' or the 'Empress Waltz' were the weekly choice for several seasons, and seemed a very apt choice for the deeds of 'derring do' which were shortly to follow. After this a short warming up period for competitors' machines was permitted. Spectators crowded the outside of the 'pits' area to

ERRATUM: Apologies for this error which has come to light after printing: Pg. 26, bottom col. 1 please add: from several local gas works constituted the top dressing or: Bottom col. 2 please add: watch these proceedings and hopefully to get their favourites

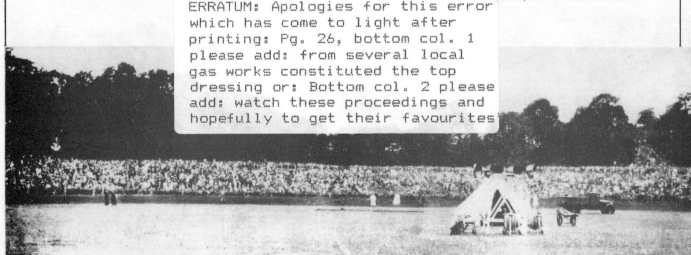

autographs. At this first meeting, all competitors were out in the open, but due to a cloudburst during the afternoon, covered accommodation for rider and machines was provided the following week. Each rider then had a covered corrugated iron pen for his machines as a guard against inclement weather.

After a few races, when the track had become somewhat rutted, an interval for smoothing and grading was necessary. Originally this was performed by the ten ton steam roller mentioned earlier, but owing to the length of time this took to complete the operation, it was soon replaced by a large new recovery vehicle. This towed three lengths of railway line angled at 45 degrees and covered most of the track width in one lap and took a mere two minutes per lap. The angled pieces of line caused most of the displaced cinders to be channelled back towards the inner edge of the track and spread nice and evenly.

Between races, the manual rakers did what they could in the time available, but the mechanical raker had to be used at frequent intervals, usually after every three or four races. This type of mechanical raker is still in use at all modern speedways.

During handicap races the 'scratch' man had to overhaul his earlier starting fellows inside four laps. This necessitated a lot of manouvering and passing, to the delight of the fans.

Early races and riders

At the first meeting, a cloudburst during the afternoon caused consternation amongst the Australian 'star' riders who were not accustomed to racing in the rain. Less experienced English competitors revelled in the wet conditions and were triumphant in most races. Ron Johnson, Sig Schlamm and Charlie Datson were the three Australian riders concerned. Johnson continued racing in England very successfully for about twenty five years but the other two returned home after only one season in this country.

During this first Crystal Palace meeting, a mini test match against Australia was raced. In a series of match races Lionel Wills (Rudge) beat Ron Johnson (Harley).

Roger Frogley beat Charlie Datson and Sig Schlam (Douglas) beat Les Blakeborough (Cotton).

In the final between the three winners Roger Frogley (Rudge) was successful from Lionel Wills (Rudge).

The first real full Test Match was raced at Wimbledon in 1929.

Scratch races, wherein all riders started on equal terms, had to be carefully vetted so that only riders of equal ability started in each race. These were usually elimination races prior to an end of meeting grand final. The winner received a cup or other trophy. Match races between two 'star' riders were very popular with the

patrons, particularly if one was a local favourite.

Back in 1928, during the formative year, races were won at comparatively slow speeds. In fact a special trophy was put up for competition between the first four Palace riders to win races at more than 39 mph. The four were A.R. (Buster) Frogley, his brother Roger, Joe Francis and Arthur Willimott.

Roger Frogley

The Frogley brothers both rode Frogley special machines which were basically 1928 Dirt Track Rudge motors, much modified to Frogley design and specification. They marketed these machines for some time prior to the more sophisticated Douglas, Rudge and Wallis machines becoming available in quantity.

Joe Francis changed from his trusted Ariel to a Douglas about this time. Arthur Willimott used one of the earlier Douglas machines which left something to be desired. They were altered in 1929 to begin a very successful period in their history.

Fewer and better machines were available in 1929 and many of the original machines disappeared from speedway. Two popular Palace riders, Ron Johnson and Arthur

Willimott had fingers severed as a result of track mishaps. Both caught their fingers in the back chains of their Douglas machines whilst attempting adjustments when on the move. Arthur never did ride again, but Ron continued until mid 1950, when a serious accident confined him to a wheelchair. A national fund amongst spectators paid for Ron to return to Australia where he still lives, now aged 80 years.

Ron Johnson

Ron Johnson was the first Crystal Palace track record holder, covering four laps at 40.07 mph. All records in those days were quoted in miles per hour as against the modern tendency to quote seconds (or part thereof). Other records quickly followed when weather conditions permitted somewhat faster racing. All record breakers at the Palace received an extra cash award and a trophy for their efforts.

Joe Francis

Marching along together

Racing in those early days was predeced by a parade of track officials in white coats, track rakers in orange and black jerseys and St John's Ambulance crew in black and white uniforms. This formed a spectacular opening as they marched to their posts to the strains of 'Marching Along Together'. Handicap races with up to six competitors per race usually opened the proceedings. The star rider was on the scratch mark, and the other riders were given anything up to twenty seconds start according to ability and experience.

Starting procedures

'Pusher-offers' were employed to start the racing machines since self-starters or kickstarters were discarded to reduce weight. One pusher was allowed per machine.

Amongst the more illustrious and successful competitors during the inaugural season of 1928 were Ron Johnson, Roger and Buster Frogley, Joe Francis, Lionel Wills, Triss Sharp, Frank North, Lew Lancaster, Gordon Cobbold, Arthur Willimott, Jack Barrett, Wally Harris, Wilf Horley, Len Bell, Bill Delaney, Bill Bragg, Dick Bellamy, Billy Coglan and quite a few others. These were all Palace contract riders, though many other celebrated performers from other tracks were also invited to compete in these early meetings.

This was the best that could be devised at that time although it did lead to disputes and controversy. One of these pushers was Crystal Palace Foundation member Bert Slough, who now in his 80th year recalls with joy those happy-go-lucky days of 1928. He still gets very voluble at the mention of Crystal Palace speedway in those never to be forgotten days.

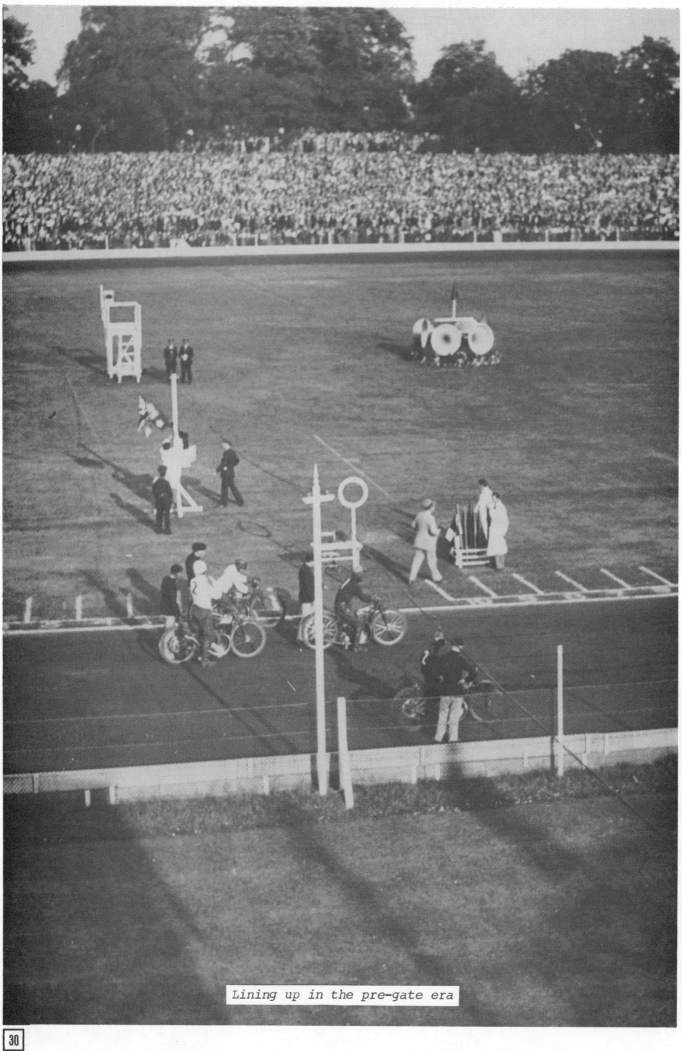

Lining up in the pre-gate era

Bert confided to me recently that he was paid the princely sum of 3/9d for his three hour stint of pushing. Having undergone a period of pushing myself I can vouch that it is a very strenuous and arduous occupation and I am sure Bert earned every penny of his fee, particularly when a machine refused to start quickly.

Some machines were easier to start than others, the Scott being relatively easy, but the Douglas and James were notoriously difficult. Aided by the pusher, some riders soon mastered the art of the 'run and bump' start. Others never did, however, and this then became a very strenuous time for the push starters.

Push starts were regarded as one of the banes of early dirt track racing. They showed up the weakness of some pushers to the detriment of a few competitors. This was partly remedied by the introduction of the 'Rolling Start'. Here, the riders toured slowly round the track until approximately twenty yards from the official start line and the starting Marshall dropped his flag when all riders were roughly in line. Competitors could then accelerate violently as they crossed the start line to commence a race. However, human nature being what it is, and coupled with nervous tension and exuberance, one can well imagine the consternation of officials who tried to ensure that no rider stole a march on his fellow competitors. Re-run races were frequent and often frustrating. Still, as nothing better was then available this form of starting races had to be endured by the long-suffering fans.

Clutch starts were introduced in 1930. These replaced most of the earlier haphazard starting procedures and continued until mid 1932 when a starting gate with tapes was invented. This was on the lines of those now in use at horse racing tracks.

Fred Mockford at the new starting gate with Stan Greatrex, George Newton and Harry Shepherd

It was invented by Fred Mockford and Palace rider Harry Shepherd, and was a rubber activated, hand-operated device used at the discretion of the starting Marshall. The later starting gate was electrically operated and controlled by the A-CU referee. These starting innovations resulted in improved track records. The new gate did at least ensure that all riders were stationary immediately prior to the tapes being raised by the unseen A-CU official. A record which stood for several years was set in 1928 by Lionel Wills of path racing fame, who covered the one lap standing start at a speed of 41.35 mph.

Leg trailing and broadsiding

The large banked Crystal Palace track encourged two very distinct types of rider. The first was the 'foot forward' type who normally rode as close as possible to the inner edge of the track thereby covering the least possible distance. (Incidentally, the official length of the track was 449 yards, measured three feet from the inner edge). The second type of rider was the more spectacular 'leg trail' rider, who plotted a longer and somewhat faster course nearer the outer periphery of the track. This style encouraged violent broadsiding, so beloved by the old time enthusiasts.

Leg-trail

On your bike!

Not all the interest was in the riders. Spectators were also interested in the many and varied machines being raced and the personal adaptations made by some riders. In 1928 some forty different makes of bike were used at the Palace. By 1929, some twenty-five different manufacturers offered special dirt track models in their current catalogues,

DOUGLAS

varying in price from £58 to more than £120. This may seem cheap to present-day readers, but it is well to remember that a young person's wage at that time was only in the region of two or three pounds per week. This then represented about twenty weeks' wages for a new bike. Today a new speedway machine is around £2,000, which represents an equivalent cost. The following

ZENITH

Foot-forward

machines were available in 1929 (and all appeared on the Palace track at some time or other): AJS, Ariel, BSA, Coventry Eagle, Coventry Victor, Cotton, Calthorpe, Douglas Excelsior, Harley, Indian, James, Matchless, Norton, New Imperial, OEC, P & M, P & P, Rudge Sunbeam, Scott, Triumph, Velocette, Wallis and Zenith.

RUDGE

BSA

Thus, prospective riders had a very wide choice of machines. The most popular being the Rudge, Douglas, Scott, Harley and Wallis. Most of the others did not appear for very long and fell into obscurity for reasons of cost or lack of performance. Today only four makes of speedway machine are manufactured, Weslake and Godden being made in England, Jawa in

JAMES

Czechoslovakia and the new much fancied GM from Italy.

During the ensuing years the machines which were still available tended to favour those riders who preferred the 'foot forward' method of riding. The luckless 'leg trail' adherents were gradually ousted from the scene. A few persisted until the outbreak of World War II, but nowadays one

seldom sees exponents of this scintillating and exuberant form of riding. This is a great pity.

Since the bikes could not be ridden to and from the track, being devoid of brakes, mudguards, lights etc., they had to be transported either on the back of a car, on a trailer or sidecar. This was fine if one could afford both a car and racing bikes. Some riders garaged

SCOTT

their machines adjacent to the track. At the Palace, bikes could be housed in the revamped stables up against the railway embankment at the Anerley end of the stadium. This was always a popular meeting place for young riders. Two riders regularly pushed their machines to and from their Croydon homes, a distance of five or six miles each way!

Dope and down draught carburettors

All riders experimented with fuel mixtures, (petrol, 'dope' or benzol from the gasworks, etc) in an effort to coax more horse power from their machines. They used larger rear tyres, down draught carburettors, four-valve engines, and many dodges to reduce unnecessary weight. The possibilities were almost endless.

As a result of all this experimentation the A-CU ruling body instigated certain rules which had to be adhered to. These included the standardisation of compression ratios, standard patterns of rear tyres, a ban on alcoholic mixtures and a return to pump fuel only. These restrictions had little effect overall but due to complaints of excessive noise from residents in Thicket Road and Anerley Park, silencers were introduced for a short while. However, due to the detrimental engine performance in conjunction with other rules, these soon died a natural death. Silencers were however re-introduced and are compulsory on all machines on British speedways to this day. The raucous crackle of racing engines and the smell of burnt Castrol R oil, the very lifeblood of all the early dirt track enthusiasts, is no more.

Up the stairs and flying high

I well remember following Triss Sharp, the Palace Captain, as he drove a 30 CWT Chevrolet truck from the Penge entrance turnstiles up the two hundred odd steps and into the Centre Transept. A quite amazing feat which was performed as an advertising stunt and also a wager. The loser was required to contribute a sizable donation to the Riders' Benevolent Fund.

The mention of Triss reminds me of another great occasion for the popular diminutive Palace idol. Following a nasty accident at Lea Bridge in a match race against Jimmy Stevens (the then Lea Bridge Captain), Triss had to undergo a lengthy period of recuperation. During his enforced track lay off, he became 21 years of age. He had a very large fan club who duly presented him with an Austin Seven sports car. Poor Triss had to be lifted into the car from his

crutches before doing a lap of honour round the track. His career as Captain did in fact continue until 1934 when the track closed and moved to New Cross. Triss' racing career was never the same at New Cross, nor indeed at Birmingham, from whence he finally hung up his leathers for good. Sadly he passed away at his Dorset home at the early age of fifty four.

Roger Frogley, Fred Mockford, Amy Johnson, and Jim Mollinson at the Herts and Essex Flying Club, Broxbourne.

The Palace ace Roger Frogley once arrived in his privately owned light aircraft and landed on the old cycle track. He then contested three match races against Gus Kuhn, the Stamford Bridge Captain, before taking off again (but only just) from the cycle track. The site is now occupied by the swimming bath complex. I think he only did it once as a ban was suddenly enforced as regards private flying over populated areas. Roger was a keen and dedicated veteran member of the Dirt Track Riders' Association who sadly passed away in mid 1970.

Alf Coles works on a bike

Workshop

Workshop facilities at the Palace were commenced in 1929 in the old stables, then situated up against the railway embankment at the Thicket Road end of the stadium grounds under the supervision of George Wallis. Riders with limited mechanical knowledge could have their bikes tuned to a high standard by a professional. George left after a short period to concentrate on the manufacture of his celebrated Wallis machines of which about 2,000 were made. The workshop facilities continued under Tommy Hall (himself a celebrated rider) and Alf Coles. They continued at New Cross after the closure of the Palace track.

Jack Barnet's mode of transport, 1929

Alf's brother, Len Coles, maintains three 1929 dirt track Douglas machines in pristine condition at his home near Crystal Palace. These are often raced in veteran events. As there are only very few of these old 'Duggies' still in existence they are prized possessions. Originally they cost £85 each, but I believe collectors will pay up to £6,000 for a good example today.

Programmes

At the top of the Penge entrance steps were two large tables where you could buy programmes for sixpence each and copies of the 'Auto'. This motoring magazine contained an eight page sepia supplement of dirt track news and pictures. Good value at twopence a copy and a very popular publication. After about four years this disappeared from the scene. Incredibly, I came come across some copies in the Western desert during World War II! Copies are rare and most desirable collectors' items. I only know of one fan who has a dozen copies of the 'Auto'. These give accounts of all London meetings together with several photographs of celebrated riders.

I have also recently seen a collection of about a hundred Crystal Palace programmes from the opening date up to 1934. This complete set of the 128 Crystal Palace programmes is a valuable rarity and is probably the only complete set in existence, belonging to an Aylesbury collector.

The Palace programme had 16 glossy pages with a five colour cover, and kept this format right up to number 128 in 1934 when the track closed down. Page 2 featured race times in 1/5th seconds showing lap and race speeds for the benefit of amateur timekeepers and other interested parties. Page 3 always showed a list of all officials

CRYSTAL PALACE SPEEDWAY

Promoters LONDON MOTOR SPORTS, Ltd.

Thrills and Speed   OPENING MEETING

SATURDAY, MAY 19, 1928 AT 3.30

GREAT INTERNATIONAL MATCH

AUSTRALIA v. ENGLAND   £100 PRIZE

NEXT MEETING SATURDAY, MAY 26, 1928 AT 7

6d.

were taken up by details of races and finals.

When the track was reopened in 1938 a six page 'flimsy' programme in black and white only was used, no doubt in an effort to save costs. The list of officials was still included, as was the list of competing riders, but no mention of machines was made since only one make of machine was being used - the British J.A.P. machine. The word 'Speedway' rather than 'dirt track racing' was always used on Crystal Palace programmes which helped popularise this term.

Originally the term 'Speedway' was the trade mark of the then governing body of all speedway sport. It came into more common use about 1932.

Palace stars

RON JOHNSON
was a recognised star when he joined Crystal Palace in 1928. He remained a top class rider with London Motor Sports until an accident confined him to a wheelchair in the early 1950's. He started racing here on a Harley, but soon changed to Douglas, Rudge, Wallis and Norton machines.

including Sir Henry Buckland, London Motor Sports (the promoters), A-CU officials, the Timekeeper, Announcer, Doctor, St. Johns Ambulance Crew etc.

Page 4 listed competing riders, their machines, and parent track. Most of course were locals from the Crystal Palace Motor Cycle Racing Club.

Page 5 detailed record holders' times and speeds. A page entitled 'Palace Matters' was always presented by the two promoters Mr. Mockford and Mr. Smith.

There was a page of supporters' club news which usually had a list of club souvenirs for sale such as photos, scarves, hats etc. Another page gave bus, tram and train services to all parts of London. The inside back cover was retained for a calendar of forthcoming events. The middle pages frequently had photos of Palace favourites. Other pages

Who is that masked man? (See p. 41)

Alex Peel

Joe Francis   *Wally Lloyd*   *Wally(Nobby)Key*   *Arthur(Buster)Frogley*

JOE FRANCIS from Sidcup was 'capped' for England in several Test Matches. He started on an Ariel, but later rode Douglas, Rudge and Wallis machines. Joe died recently in the Isle of Man at the age of 78.

TRISS SHARP, proprietor of a motor business at South Croydon, was the undisputed 'leg trailing' idol of Palace fans. Diminutive of stature, he became the Captain of Palace teams from 1930 to 1934. He retired when the track closed in 1934, but made two unsuccessful attempts to come back with New Cross and Birmingham. He started riding on an AJS, then a Calthorpe, Douglas, Rudge and Wallis.

ARTHUR WILLIMOTT, also from the Sidcup area, started on an HRD machine, but soon gained fame on Douglas and Rudge machines. His career was ended following the severing of several fingers in a track mishap.

JACK BARRETT, a Douglas fanatic who raced regularly for several seasons, was a onetime track record holder. He still resides in South London.

ROGER FROGLEY was the first British star rider and raced in several Test Matches against Australia. He retired when the Palace track closed to concentrate on his aviation business at Hoddesdon (Herts) and made an unsuccessful comeback at New Cross in 1936.

ARTHUR (BUSTER) FROGLEY, brother of Roger, later captained Wembley where he raced for several seasons. He was a saxophone player and a newsagent also at Hoddesdon (Herts). Sadly 'Buster' died recently aged 80. Another link with the past now lost forever.

BILL BRAGG, a motor cycle engineer from Brixton, and **DICK BELLAMY**, who ran a tyre business at Waddon, both rode Coventry Eagle machines. Both later transferred to Stamford Bridge speedway.

ERIC HAMBRIDGE from Surbiton and **'JIMMY' JAMES** both rode and persevered with the very cumbersome James machine with mixed fortunes.

WILF HORLEY, manager of a large Croydon motor cycle showroom, rode a beautifully prepared Scott machine for some years. He was an early one lap record holder and a great favourite.

'BUSTER' BUCKLAND, a junior relative of the Palace General Manager, raced regularly in 1928 and 1929. He later transferred to Exeter where he was very successful for some years.

LIONEL WILLS, heir to the tobacco fortunes, rode very well for two or three seasons. He was one of very few genuine 'amateurs'. He retired to concentrate on the family business.

BASIL DUDLEY rode under a pseudonym (Greathurst) in order to try and nullify parental disapproval.

TOMMY HALL later became Palace chief mechanic, with **ALF COLES** in the communal workshops.

GEORGE LOVICK, of Penge, and **BRIAN DONKIN** were also team members.

Clem Mitchell   *Harry Shepherd*   *George Newton*   *Gus Kuhn*

HARRY SHEPHERD, the starting gate inventor, rode for the Palace until 1934. He then went to Bristol and later New Cross.

KARL PUGH was a civil servant who was compelled by his bosses to stop racing. He rode a D.O.T. machine for some time.

LES BLAKEBOROUGH, a retired civil servant, later joined the Stamford Bridge team where he was very successful for several seasons.

After 1930, several Northern and Midland tracks closed. There was also an influx of some foreign riders from Europe, South Africa and America. These factors led to team changes at the Palace, who were joined by –

WALLY (NOBBY) KEY from Wales,
TOM FARNDON from Coventry,
WALLY LLOYD from Birmingham,
STAN BAINES from High Beech,
KAI ANDERSEN from Denmark,
WALTER RYLE from Denmark,
CLEM MITCHELL from Australia,
and **WILL NICHOLAS** from South Africa, who died in 1933 in a motoring accident on Salisbury Plain.

GEORGE NEWTON from Ash Vale, Aldershot, was one who quickly reached dizzy heights at the Palace. Sadly he died in November 1984 aged 74.

There were also quite a few good riders at the Palace who never made team status for one reason or another, like **WALLY HARRIS** who still lives near the Palace at Portland Road, South Norwood. He could not spare time from his business to travel mid-week with the team. There were also literally dozens of novice riders under training, and all clamouring for rides.

FRANK NORTH of Selhurst, confided to me recently that he was paid not to win, but to thrill the crowds with his fence scraping broadsides and to shower as many fans as he could with damp black cinders. How well he used to do it too! In full flight, Frank was an awe-inspiring sight, and though he frequently fell, he always seemed to have the sympathy of the crowd. He is still working in his small engineering workshop, though now over 80 years of age, still tuning machines for less knowledgeable riders. Thanks for the memories, Frank!

A few others who rode regularly for some years, yet never quite made the grade were **BILL RICHARDSON**, (Douglas), **LEN BELL** (Zenith), **BILL DELANEY** (Douglas), **'SPARKS' BURGESS** (BSA), **JIM WILLMOTT** (Rudge) and **LOUIS BULL** (Douglas) who had quite a meteoric rise to fame before a nasty accident caused him to quit the sport.

Women riders -
Discrimination on Wheels

One of the best riders at the Palace Dirt Track in the late 1920's was Fay Taylour. She was one of five women who regularly rode at the Palace track. In particular, Eva Asquith, Barbara 'Babs' Neild and Fay could hold their own with their male contemporaries.

However, their reign came to an end in 1930 when all women riders were banned by the Auto Cycle Union, the governing body for all speedway sport. This followed an accident involving a woman rider who fell off whilst riding at another track. Unfortunately, the rider behind ran over her, causing chronic chest injuries. The St Johns Ambulance Brigade created headlines by having to strip her to the waist in full view of the grandstand.

FAY TAYLOUR campaigned for several years to get the female riders reinstated, without success. Her desire for the thrills of the track were later partly satisfied by becoming one of the pioneers of banger car racing, together with other successes at road racing, hill climbing, time trials and on grand prix racing circuits. She passed away recently at her Dorset home following a long illness.

To millions of racing fans she was 'The Cinders Queen', 'The Dublin Dynamo' or 'Ireland's Whirlwind'. But Fay Taylour preferred the simple, down to earth title she gave herself - 'Women's Racing Champion of the World'.

In 1928 the promoters refused to let Fay race. So, she hid her copper curls under a leather helmet and slipped in among a group of men riders practicing at the Crystal Palace track. "They were too busy falling off to notice me. But when the promoter came along and ordered 'that lad' to be called off the track, he got a shock when I took my helmet off." She was such a good rider that the promoter was persuaded to sign her up.

"I wasn't a women's lib pioneer," Fay insisted. "'But I was a rebel. If somebody - especially a man - said I couldn't do a thing, it made me just the more determined to do it."

Fay Taylour

EVA ASQUITH became good enough for the Leeds Team, and raced several matches against selected male opponents at the Palace track. She still lives in North Yorkshire where she is an enthusiastic rose grower.

DOT COWLEY was the daughter of a famous motor cycle racing family.

The other regular women riders were **BABS NIELD,** and **VERA HOLE** from Somerset who became known as 'Sunny Somerset'. She had three brothers who all rode for Bristol in pre World War II days.

Fay Taylour and Eva Askquith say, "push off!"

Dot Cowley

Babs Nield

C.P. Track Trophy

This trophy was inaugurated in 1929 and it involved a series of races involving Palace riders only. The trophy was donated by the Palace trustees. It was valued at more than 500 guineas, even in those days, and must have represented a King's ransom to the winner.

Originally only twelve riders contested the series, but later it was expanded to include the fastest sixteen on the books. All had to have won races at the track at speeds of more than 40 mph, which meant that virtually any one of the contestants could ultimately win the trophy.

The inaugural winner was Triss Sharp, but the trophy contined to be contested until the track closed in 1934, ending in the capable hands of Tom Farndon.

Tom Farndon

A large Easter Monday crowd at the Palace, 1932.

SPEEDWAY LEAGUES

Until mid-1929 interest in speedway had been maintained, but clearly something more was needed in order to maintain momentum. The country was geographically split in two. Two leagues were formed for teams of six riders each. The Northern League of about twenty teams failed to fulfill all its matches and the final results were declared void. This was largely due to the later closure of a few tracks which could not meet their financial commitments.

The Southern League, of which the Palace was one of the founder members, consisted of around sixteen teams. At the end of the first season the Palace team was in fourth place. A creditable start to an innovation which really fired the public imagination as nothing had done to date. Nine London tracks competed together with those from Coventry, two Birmingham circuits, Southampton and one of the Leicester tracks.

The Palace team was Triss Sharp, George Lovick, Brian Donkin, Arthur Willimott, Joe Francis and Jack Barrett.

Crowds increased, supporters' clubs were started at all tracks, and generally the fans became very partisan. In this inaugural league, all matches were run over nine heats only, but this was increased to thirteen in subsequent years, and remains so to this day. Thirteen heats often prevents matches ending in a draw.

Prior to this league commencing, a trial team event was raced between Crystal Palace and a team of three riders from Marine Gardens Speedway, Edinburgh. The Scottish team of Drew McQueen, Geo McKenzie and Norrie Isbister, were all mounted on the new Royal Enfield machines then making their debut. As expected, the Palace team were the winners, but six-rider teams were later instigated.

A six-man team from Belle Vue, Manchester, raced a trial event in 1929 against Palace riders who occupied first and second positions in each of the nine heats, to record a perfect score: 45 points to 9. Thus league racing started, and continues with little change up to the present day.

Due to the closure of some tracks and the inclusion of 'star' riders, most teams, including the Palace, underwent considerable change. All were strengthened with the influx of riders from the defunct tracks which changed the make up of teams which had previously featured mainly local riders. Thus in 1932 a new league was started – the National League. This embraced such Northern tracks as were still solvent and wished to compete.

* See Appendix for League Tables.

Nobby Key, Joe Francis, Harry Shepherd, Tom Farndon, Alf Sawford, Clem Mitchell (reserve) and Ron Johnson (Capt.)

Motor-cycle football

Sidecar polo

ROSETTES AND INNOVATION

Test Matches against Australia were also run at this time, and several of these were run at the Palace. These generated enormous interest and spectators frequently exceeded 50,000. These figures may seem huge to modern readers, but they were often exceeded at Bank Holiday meetings where 100,000 spectators were commonplace. A Crystal Palace Supporters' Club was started in 1930 and quickly grew to upwards of 20,000 regular paid-up members. These supporters paid a reduced admission charge by showing their membership card. Hats, scarves, rosettes and other favours in the Palace colours of orange and black were soon in evidence, and a colourful sight they made too.

Two supporters' club members carried a huge bell between them to arouse support from spectators and to spur on the team. This bell had previously been sited on top of the Penge entrance turnstile where it had been used to warn late night revellers of the approach of closing time. I wonder what happened to it?

The French had never been famous as a speedway nation, but did have a Frenchman riding at the Crystal Palace in 1929. Ive de Lathe rode a somewhat cumbersome Triumph machine with much greater verve than success. He travelled from Paris to ride, which must have been very expensive. He fell very frequently but fortunately without serious injury.

The Palace was famous for innovations. They even tried horse racing at the 6th speedway meeting in June 1928. Four races with four horses each took place. The riders were well known jockeys of the day attired in their gaily coloured 'silks'. The winner of each heat went into a four horse final, which, though colourful was not very spectacular. Since betting was precluded at all speedway events run under AC-U regulations, this proved to be a minority interest and a vote taken was against horse racing at future programmes.

In those far off days, few tracks operated under floodlights. So far as I know, only Stamford Bridge and White City could afford such luxury. Saturday was the regular race day at the Palace with normally a 3.30 p.m. start time. Some Saturday, and a few Wednesday, evening meetings with a 6.30 p.m. start were held in June, July and August when summer-time daylight permitted.

What memorable days!

When other tracks raced league matches at the Palace, crowds were often enormous because the visiting

Midget car racing

teams brought hordes of their own supporters by coach or bus. A one shilling tram ticket enabled others to travel to and from the Palace from almost all parts of the Metropolis. Crowds from Wembley, Wimbledon, West Ham, Stamford Bridge, Lea Bridge, White City, Haringay and Kings Oak (High Beech) in Epping Forest could thus make the return journey - a bob for an all-day ticket.

From 1930, team racing became a specialised art at the Palace speedway. Team members who regularly rode together developed an almost uncanny knowledge of their partner's style. These regular team pairs annually contested a 'Best Pairs Championship' which has continued even to the present day. The Palace team comprised several notable pairs - Ron Johnson and Joe Francis who rode together for years, even after the Palace track closed. Tom Farndon and 'Nobby' Key also rode together for a long time until the untimely death of poor Tom in 1935.

In an effort to offset the increasing weekly rent levied on speedway by the Crystal Palace trustees, several other types of motorised sports were tried at the Sydenham stadium:

Motor cycle football

was quite exciting, but did not catch the public eye to any degree. Also, as there were only four other clubs interested, diversified competition was somewhat difficult and this was not staged after 1928.

Sidecar polo

was also played for a short time as an interval attraction.

Sidecar speedway

thrilled spectators for two or three seasons, culminating in the Crystal Palace championships of 1929 and 1930 before being excluded from the programmes altogether. The dearth of

competitors hastened its demise, since the competitors were the same, as contested the path racing events which were still being run.

Midget car racing

on the speedway track lasted about half a season before being abandoned. The crowd appeal for this expensive and exhilarating sport was sadly lacking. The leading drivers were Walter Mackereth, C.S. Dellow, Jean Reville from France and a Mexican called 'Spike' Rhiando. The list of drivers was frequently very short which precluded much regular competition.

An annual twenty lap speedway event was started which proved to be of great fun for both riders and spectators. All riders were involved in at least one pit stop for fuel and oil since the bikes were fitted with very small tanks, sufficient for only eight or ten laps of the track. Incidentally, this type of race has recently been revived at several modern speedways.

Track record attempts were always popular, with a trophy and cheque being presented by a popular celebrity of the day to the successful riders. A wealthy

Crystal Palace supporter offered a huge silver cup to the first Palace contract rider to cover three laps of the track (from a standing start) in less than one minute.

Several riders came quite close during the previous years, but in 1933 Harry 'Shep' Shepherd took the silverware and cheque with a time of 59.8 seconds. After several successful seasons, Harry retired to Australia where he works as a master builder. His brother told me recently that he was still fit and well, though now over 80 years of age.

Track records have been mentioned earlier but below will be found a comprehensive list right from 1928. These are divided into classes:-

First lap standing start

The first holder was Lionel Wills with a speed of 41.35 mph, which stood for about four years when, under the new clutch start rules, Ron Johnson raised the record speed to 42 mph. In 1934 the mercurial Tom Farndon pushed this up to an incredible 43.16 mph. Tom eventually held all the Palace records at the time of the track's closure in 1934.

One lap flying start

The record speed was invariably achieved on either the second, third, or fourth lap of a four-lap race. Ron Johnson was the first record holder at 43.6 mph. Triss Sharp later recorded 45.01 mph, and Harry Shepherd achieved 45.9 mph during a three laps in one minute spectacular. Finally, Tom Farndon returned an unbeatable speed of 49.7 mph just before the track closed.

Four lap clutch start

The record for this was originally set in 1928 by Ron Johnson with a speed of over 40.07 mph. It was improved on over the years by several riders in turn: Roger Frogley at 41.69 mph, Triss Sharp at 42.5 mph, Stan Baines 42.68 mph, Jack Barrett 42.90 mph, Ron Johnson again at 44.68 mph and finally Tom Farndon at 45.89 mph.

Tom also set up a one-off record for four laps with a flying start at 47.70 mph and thus Tom held all records in 1934. Unfortunately he was tragically killed at New Cross in 1935 so he remains, posthumously, the holder of all the Palace records.

London riders' championship

This was started at the Palace and was in effect a mini world championship. Contested by sixteen riders (two from each of the London tracks) it was held in very high esteem by both riders and spectators alike.

The first winner was Jack Ormston of Wembley in 1930, receiving a trophy and a large cheque. Joe Francis of Crystal Palace succeeded in 1931, and another Palace rider Tom Farndon won again in 1932 and 1933. He also succeeded in 1934 after the team had moved to New Cross. The London championship is still challenged to this day, but with the smaller number of tracks now operating in the Metropolis, it has assumed a much less important role in the current speedway calendar.

Since metrication was happily almost unknown in those days, all records were announced in English measurements. These were generally set when the riders were blessed with -

A nicely graded smooth track.

Damp (though not wet) weather which promotes better 'breathing' by the high revving engines.

A machine tuned to mechanical perfection.

The right mental and physical attitude.

DESTRUCTION AND DESOLATION

By 1934, fewer spectator delights were being held either within the Palace or within the spacious grounds. Path racing and speedway regularly attracted large crowds. Unfortunately, the annual rent and rates increased dramatically to approaching £1,000 per week. An application to install floodlights, and so permit evening racing had also been turned down by the Palace trustees. These factors led the promoters, London Motor Sports, to clear out lock, stock and barrel to New Cross. Path racing and speedway at the Palace ceased, as did the motor boat racing on the North Tower lake.

Apart from concerts and organ recitals in the Palace itself, there were now few events to attract the patrons through the turnstiles. Even the previously popular Bank Holiday extravaganzas seemed to be poorly attended. One realises that by 1934, with motor cycles becoming cheaper, and the advent of the £100 family car, people tended to visit the country and seaside at holiday periods. Thus income at the Palace dwindled rapidly.

A few 'amateur' tracks operated in and around London and provided excellent training facilities for young riders. Dagenham, Smallford (St. Albans), Barnet, Romford, Watford, 'California in England' (Wokingham) all supplied riders to the more prosperous professional tracks.

On the evening of 30th November 1936, the Palace was burnt to the ground in one of the greatest fires seen in London since the Great Fire of 1666. Flames were first noticed by night security patrols at about 6.30 - 7.00 pm. After a short while, they had to admit that the blaze was beyond their limited fire fighting resources. Just why these resources were so very limited is open to conjecture, since this was the third or fourth fire in the eighty years of the Palace's existence. However, an alarm call was eventually made to Penge Fire Station, who raced to the scene. A quick survey of the fire convinced the officer in charge that his small team would require considerable assistance. Calls were sent to fire stations throughout London, Croydon, Sutton and surrounding areas. The sound of one fire appliance from Croydon aroused little interest for my friend and I who were at the time busily tuning our racing bikes in readiness for the coming weekend meeting. When a further eight engines roared past in quick succession, we simply had to investigate. My friend lived in Addiscombe, near the Morland crossroads, and from there we could clearly see the glow in the night sky. My friend's mother, who was at the time listening to the radio, heard the programme interruption announcing 'the Crystal Palace Fire'. We jumped on one of the bikes and raced up to the Palace, but were stopped about half a mile from the scene where we parked the bike in Church Road and managed to get a little closer on foot. By now the crowds were enormous and increasing by the minute. Some 64 appliances were hosing the fire with little effect. Being on top of Sydenham Hill, water pressure was not very great. The North tower lake was quickly drained and long pipes were laid through the grounds to the reservoir near the maze, and also to the Penge entrance lakes. We had a good view

from Central Hill, near the Gips
Hill Police Station, this being th
nearest we could get. Considerin
the size of the building, th
severity of the conflagration an
the difficulty in obtaining
sufficient water supply, .it i
amazing that no one was hur
Molten glass ran in Crystal Palac
parade and down Anerley Hill. Thi
filled the tramway tracks an
caused the trams to stop and t
turned around at Anerley Statior
over half a mile away.

The fire burned all night. Nothing remained save a huge mass of twisted metal, although miraculously, the two water towers were virtually unharmed. Clearing up after the fire took many days. Most of the metal framework was cut up and sold as scrap to the German firm Krupps of Essen, which was surprising in view of the fact that war clouds were already gathering.

Lloyds, the insurance underwriters, paid out £110,000 in compensation within a week, which leaves one wondering how thoroughly the investigations were carried out. This figure was a fraction of its monetary and emotional value, and the Palace was sorely missed by the millions who had enjoyed it. The whole complex became known as the 'white elephant' of South London.

The North and South Towers were demolished during the early part of the 1939/45 war, as they were considered to be too good a landmark for enemy bombers.

The once popular speedway stadium became ghostly, unused and deteriorating. Grass and weeds soon started to appear, the paintwork peeled on the stands - a sight of utter desolation.

Gordon Cobbold and Triss Sharpe

All fall down!

CRYSTAL PALACE

27th MAY, 1939
CRYSTAL PALACE
v.
BRISTOL
NATIONAL TROPHY

3D.

REBIRTH OF PALACE SPEEDWAY

Late in 1937, a new promoter applied for a licence to run speedway at the Crystal Palace in the then newly formed Speedway Second Division.

The track was cleared of weeds and grass and the racing surface was found to be in excellent condition. The stands were refurbished and the general aspect cleaned up in readiness for an early start in the summer of 1938. The new staff of riders consisted solely of novice and first year recruits. The stars of yesteryear were precluded from this ostensibly training track league. Thus a completely new set of names appeared, and the new Crystal Palace team was a team of 'unknowns'. A period of training and practicing produced several very promising juniors, some of whom eventually rose to National League (First Division) status.

The original concept of this Second Division was soon altered to permit several better known riders to compete in the teams. Others emerged from retirement and the whole hurly burly of speedway was re-born.

The 1938 Palace team was captained by Les Trim, a local rider, and included Bob Lovell, Mick Mitchell, Keith Harvey, Archie Windmill, Jack Bibby, Lloyd Goffe, George Gower, Vic Weir, Les Gregory and Geo Dykes. The team did not enjoy the success, nor the support, of the original Crystal Palace team, though a supporters' club was formed. The League was comprised of only ten teams, but at least it was a start (or a re-start).

In an attempt to stir the memories of pre-war devotees, here are pen-pictures of the best Palace riders:

Keith Harvey, orginally from South Africa, became a regular Stamford Bridge Rider in the late 1920's before going to Norwich prior to joining Crystal Palace. He became very consistent at the Palace. He owned a large motor cycle emporium at Stockwell. He continued after the war at New Cross and was still riding when well past the age of fifty.

Bob Lovell had some experience of Midlands tracks and his exuberant leg trailing style gained him a host of admirers. He continued riding after the war for a variety of other tracks and was President of the Veteran Dirt Track Riders Association (VDTRA) in 1982, and still rides in veteran events.

Les Gregory joined the Palace as a junior and soon became a regular and reliable team rider. He is also a keen VDTRA member.

Archie Windmill was a pre-war Hackney rider of some repute prior to racing at the Palace. At 6' 2" he must have been one of the tallest riders in the business. Using his very long legs to the best advantage he was a most difficult rider to pass. He continued at Hackney for some years after the war and is now an active member of the VDTRA.

Lloyd Goffe of Reading, had been a youthful competitor at the now defunct California in England track on an old AJS of dubious ancestry. On his debut at the Palace, he won his first four races on a seven year old Rudge and thereafter became a steady scorer. He continued after the war for many seasons at Harringay and later Wimbledon.

George Gower commenced at New Cross as a junior rider before joining the Palace in 1939 where he rode steadily without any spectacular results. He later returned to New Cross and then moved to West Ham. More recently he was badly crushed in a tractor accident at Leicester, where he was track maintenance supervisor. Nowadays he is confined to a wheelchair but is still an enthusiastic member of the VDTRA.

Mick Mitchell was a local novice who made good at the Palace. His exciting leg trailing style made him very popular. He continued after the war at New Cross, Swindon and Hull with considerable success.

Les Trim, the captain, had ridden for quite a time on various London amateur tracks. Never a world beater, but nonetheless a very competent performer at this level of competition.

Geo Dykes was previously with Nottingham but came to the Palace prior to the war.

Vic Weir rode for Crystal Palace in 1939 then continued in the West Midlands until retiring.

Jack Bibby, from Australia, met with mixed fortunes at the Palace before returning home at the outbreak of World War II. He should not be confused with the more recent Crayford rider of the same name who came from Southend on Sea after a lengthy spell at Iwade training tack in Kent.

This second era of racing was frequently exciting and unpredictable but never quite reached the dizzy heights of previous years, and though the crowds were smaller, the track did remain solvent. The advent of World War II brought all racing to a halt in September 1939.

One additional meeting, sponsored by ENSA for the entertainment of troops, was run in 1940 and was the very last time the track was used for racing. Subsequently it was taken over by the War Department and used as a military tank park with consequent disastrous results. Very little was left when the hostilities ceased, and no attempt was made to restart speedway again at the Crystal Palace.

A concrete road racing circuit was laid down and used for about twenty years by motor cars and motor cycles, but my knowledge of this circuit is very limited and in fact other more knowledgable scribes will cover the subject better.

The site of the original speedway ground is now occupied by the National Sports Centre stadium. The present stands occupy much the same positions as the two original wooden stands. Until 1983, a small portion of the original track was fenced off and surmounted by a bronze commemoration plaque for posterity. Sadly this has disappeared, no doubt the work of vandals. Nothing seems to be sacred these days. Is the last trace of the Crystal Palace speedway lost forever?

FACTS AND FIGURES

Ivor Creek

RIDERS' PERFORMANCES IN 1929

	Rides	Wins	Per cent
Ivor Creek	10	7	70.00
Gordon Baxter	13	7	55.84
Ron Johnson	47	25	53.19
Triss Sharp	88	42	47.72
Roger Frogley	40	18	45.00
Jack Barrett	75	33	44.00
Colin Ford	21	9	42.85
Bryan Donkin	50	21	42.00
Gus Kuhn	52	18	34.61
Wally Harris	49	16	32.65
"Tiger" Stevenson	13	4	30.77
Arthur Willimott	77	22	28.57
Len Reeve	12	3	25.00
Lewis Bull	19	4	21.03
Joe Francis	62	13	20.95
"Nobby" Key	10	2	20.00
George Lovick	63	11	17.46
Les Blakeborough	18	3	16.66
"Buster" Frogley	32	5	15.62
Frank North	36	5	13.88
Don Everness	22	3	13.63
Dick Bellamy	15	2	13.33
"Sparks" Burgess	27	3	11.11
Les Bowden	36	4	11.11
Billy Coghlan	25	2	8.00
Nick Nicol	13	1	7.68
Wilfred Horley	16	1	6.25
Steve Pullen	35	2	5.71
George Pettit	21	1	4.76
Fred Cooper	36	1	2.77

TRAVELLING FACILITIES
To the
Crystal Palace Speedway

TRAINS	SOUTHERN RAILWAY
To CRYSTAL PALACE (Low Level Station)	Twelve minutes' service from VICTORIA, via Clapham Junction, Wandsworth Common, Balham, Streatham Hill, West Norwood, Gipsy Hill
	Twelve minutes' service from LONDON BRIDGE, via New Cross Gate, Brockley, Honor Oak Park, Forest Hill, Sydenham ; or via South Bermondsey, Queen's Road, Peckham Rye, East Dulwich, North Dulwich, Tulse Hill, West Norwood, Gipsy Hill
To CRYSTAL PALACE (High Level Station)	Twenty minutes' service from ST. PAUL'S, via Elephant and Castle, Denmark Hill, Peckham Rye, Nunhead, Honor Oak, Lordship Lane, Upper Sydenham.
To CRYSTAL PALACE (Low Level Station)	Twenty minutes' service from WEST CROYDON, via South Norwood or Norwood Junction.
	Twenty minutes' service from BECKENHAM via Birkbeck.
To PENGE EAST or SYDENHAM HILL	Twenty minutes' service from Bickley, Bromley and Kent House.

COMMENCING NEXT SATURDAY, MAY 21st,
A SPECIAL TRAIN direct from COULSDON NORTH (CHEAP RETURN FARE 1/9 1st class, 1/- 3rd class) will leave at 6.0 p.m., calling at Purley (1/6 and -/10), 6.3 ; Purley Oaks (1/3 and -/8), 6.5 ; South Croydon (1/- and -/7), 6.8 ; East Croydon (-/8 and -/5), 6.11 ; Norwood Junction (-/5 and -/3), 6.15 ; arriving at CRYSTAL PALACE (Low Level) at 6.19, returning from CRYSTAL PALACE (Low Level) at 9.43, calling at Norwood Junction, 9.47 ; East Croydon, 9.52 ; South Croydon, 9.54 ; Purley Oaks, 9.57 ; Purley, 10.0 ; arriving at COULSDON NORTH at 10.3 p.m.

'BUSES	Routes 2, 3, 12a, 49c, 75d, 82b, 108, 109.
TRAMS	CRYSTAL PALACE (High Level) or CRYSTAL PALACE (Penge Entrance) from West Croydon, via Selhurst and South Norwood.
MOTOR COACHES ...	From REDHILL. Full particulars from Stanton Motors, Brook Road, REDHILL.

1929 Team - George Lovick, Brian Donkin, Arthur Willimott,
Fred Mockford (Manager), Triss Sharp, Joe Francis,
Alf Sawford, Jack Barrett.

League Tables

Southern League 1929

	P	W	D	L	Total Points
Stamford Bridge	20	17	–	1	34
Southampton	20	16	–	4	32
Coventry	20	14	–	6	28
Crystal Palace	20	11	–	9	22
Wembley	20	11	–	9	22
West Ham	20	8	–	12	16
White City	20	8	–	12	16
Harringay	20	7	–	13	14
Birmingham	20	7	–	13	14
Lea Bridge	20	6	–	14	12
Wimbledon	20	5	–	15	10

Southern League 1930

	P	W	D	L	Total Points
Wembley	24	20	1	3	41
Southampton	24	17	1	6	35
Stamford Bridge	24	16	1	7	33
Wimbledon	24	15	2	8	32
Birmingham, Hall Green	24	13	1	10	27
Coventry	24	13	1	10	27
Crystal Palace	24	11	1	12	23
Lea Bridge	24	10	1	13	21
West Ham	24	10	–	14	20
Leicester	24	8	1	15	17
High Beech, Kings Oak	24	8	1	15	17
Harringay	24	7	–	17	14
Nottingham	24	2	1	21	5

1930 Team - Triss Sharp (Capt.), Ron Johnson, "Shep" Shepherd,
Clem Mitchell, Wally Lloyd, Joe Francis, Roger Frogley, Fred Mockford (Manager).

Crystal Palace Team - London Cup Winners, 1931.
Jim Cowie, S. Pitcher, Nobby Key, Triss Sharp, Ron Johnson, Tom Farndon,
Alf Sawford, Roger Frogley (Capt.), Harry Shepherd, Joe Francis.

Southern League 1931						N.P.A Trophy Competition 1932						National League 1932				
	P	W	D	L	Total Points		P	W	D	L	Total Points		P	W	D	L	Total Points
Wembley	38	29	1	8	59	Stamford Bridge	18	16	-	2	32	Wembley	16	12	-	4	24
Stamford Bridge	38	27	-	11	54	Wembley	18	14	-	4	28	Crystal Palace	16	10	-	6	20
West Ham	38	23	-	15	46	Crystal Palace	18	12	-	6	24	Manchester	16	9	1	6	19
Crystal Palace	38	22	-	16	44	Belle Vue	18	11	-	7	22	Wimbledon	16	8	1	7	17
Wimbledon	38	19	1	18	39	West Ham	18	11	-	7	22	Stamford Bridge	16	8	-	8	16
High Beech	38	19	-	19	38	Wimbledon	18	11	-	7	22	West Ham	16	7	-	9	14
Southampton	38	18	-	20	36	Clapton	18	5	-	13	10	Coventry	16	6	-	10	12
Manchester	38	14	-	24	28	Coventry	18	5	-	13	10	Clapton	16	4	-	12	8
Lea Bridge	38	11	-	17	22	Sheffield	18	3	-	15	6	Plymouth	16	4	-	12	8
Coventry	38	8	1	29	17	Plymouth	18	2	-	16	4						

1932 Team - Alf Sawford, Joe Francis, Eric Blain, Ron Johnson,
Fred Mockford (Manager), Wally Key, Harry Shepherd,
seated - Triss Sharp, Alex Peel, George Newton, Tom Farndon

1933 Team - Triss Sharp, Joe Francis, Nobby Key, Fred Mockford (Manager), Ron Johnson, Tom Farndon, Harry Shepherd, George Newton.

National League 1933	P	W	D	L	Total Points		National League 1934	P	W	D	L	Total Points
Manchester, Belle Vue	36	31	–	5	62		Manchester, Belle Vue	30	26	–	4	52
Wimbledon	36	23	–	13	46		Wembley	30	24	–	6	48
West Ham	36	21	3	12	45		Crystal Palace/New Cross	30	20	–	10	40
Crystal Palace	36	21	–	15	42		Wimbledon	30	14	–	16	28
Clapton	36	19	3	14	41		West Ham	30	13	1	16	27
Wembley	36	19	1	16	39		Harringay	30	13	1	16	27
Coventry	36	10	2	24	22		Plymouth	30	8	2	20	18
Sheffield	36	11	–	25	22		Birmingham	30	9	–	21	18
Plymouth	36	11	–	25	22		Walthamstow	30	5	–	25	10
Nottingham	36	9	1	26	1							

1934 New Cross Team (previously Crystal Palace) -
Harry Shepherd, Roy Dook, Stan Greatrex, George Newton,
sitting Joe Francis, Tom Farndon, Fred Mockford, Ron Johnson, Nobby Key.